GENERAL CONFERENCE REPORT OF THE S.D.A., REFORM MOVEMENT

EYEWITNESS

GENERAL CONFERENCE

REPORT

OF THE S.D.A.,

REFORM MOVEMENT

MAY 7 – 31, 1951, HOLLAND

S. GUTKNECHT

INDEX

INTRODUCTION

THIS IS AN EYEWITNESS REPORT OF WHAT PARTOOK PLACE AT THE GENERAL CONFERENCE DELEGATES SESSION OF THE INTERNATIONAL MISSIONARY SOCIETY SEVENTH-DAY AD-VENTISTS CHURCH REFORM MOVEMENT, OF 7-31 MAY, 1951, IN HOLLAND, AS EXPERIENCED BY ONE OF THE GERMAN

UNION DELEGATES.

As a result of many requests from the brethren, especially from the young generation, to draft an exact report of the events and occurrences of the 1951 General Conference Assembly in Holland, I feel morally obligated with the Lord, the Omniscient, to relate what actually took place.

In debates and conversations with the "Nicolici Group," which in the year 1951 separated from the prophesized Reform of the Seventh-Day Adventists, called into existence during World War I (1914–1918), I came to the sad realization that many things had been twisted and contrived for the means of appropriating souls. It is written in Revelation 21:8 that all liars shall be found in the lake of fire that results in eternal death.

Before delving into the detailed report I would like to introduce a serious warning from the Spirit of Prophecy:

"I saw that the very spirit of perjury, that would turn truth into falsehood, good into evil, and innocence into crime, is now active. Satan exults over the condition of God's professed people. While many are neglecting their own souls, they eagerly watch for an opportunity to criticize and condemn others. All have defects of character, and it is not hard to find something that jealousy can interpret to their injury. 'Now,' say these self-constituted judges, 'we have facts. We will fasten upon them an accusation from which they cannot clear themselves.' They wait for a fitting opportunity and then produce their bundle of gossip and bring forth their tidbits

In their efforts to carry a point, persons who have naturally a strong imagination are in danger of deceiving themselves and deceiving others. They gather up unguarded expressions from another, not considering that words may be uttered hastily and hence may not reflect the real sentiments of the speaker. But those unpremeditated remarks, often so trifling as to be unworthy of notice, are viewed through Satan's magnifying glass, pondered, and repeated until molehills become mountains. Separated from God, the surmisers of evil become the sport of temptation. They scarcely know the strength of their feelings or the effect of their words. While condemning the errors of others, they indulge far greater errors themselves. Consistency is a jewel.

Is there no law of kindness to be observed? Have Christians been authorized of God to criticize and condemn one another? Is it honorable, or even honest, to win from the lips of another, under the guise of friendship, secrets which have been entrusted to him, and then turn the knowledge thus gained to his injury? Is it Christian charity to gather up every floating report, to unearth everything that will cast suspicion on the character of another, and then take delight in using it to injure him? Satan exults when he can defame or wound a follower of Christ. He is 'the accuser of our brethren.' Shall Christians aid him in his work? –Testimony Treasures, pp. 22, 23.

Those who love Jesus and understand His prayer as high priest will see himself as a responsible ambassador of Christ, and will never work towards a separation in the church of God, but will seek to remedy and restore.

The words of the apostle Paul in Romans 2:1-3 should be considered and kept in the heart as faithfully as possible by the children of God.

We have not been called to be judges, but to the service of the Gospel, as such we should not open wounds, but should bandage and cure them. It is not our work to seek out the weaknesses of character of our brothers or sisters and then relate them to the people, but we should put ourselves under the scope of the light of the Gospel. If we are shepherds and ambassadors of Christ, then we are to carry the weaknesses of the people to the sanctuary of Jesus Christ, our High Priest. Jesus says, "Blessed are the peacemakers: for they shall be called the children of God." Matthew 5:9.

David and Peter committed grave sins in our eyes, but because they were sincere and repented wholeheartedly God forgave them, hence David could continue in his administration as king, prophet, and judge.

"Therefore being a prophet, and knowing that God had

sworn with an oath to him, that of the fruit of his loins, according to the flesh, he would raise up Christ to sit on his throne. He seeing this before spake of the resurrection of Christ, that his soul was not left in hell, neither his flesh did see corruption." Acts 2:30, 31.

The behavior of the Savior with Peter is also presented as a life lesson. Even though he denied the Savior three times and rectified it by swearing and saying that he did not know Jesus, no censorship was administered on him by the Savior; no rebuke, neither church discipline, nor bellows in the streets, but a gaze. After the resurrection there was only a trying question: "Lovest thou me?"

Jesus Christ was content with his repentance and tears, thus his human weakness was forgiven. This is love; divine and saving love!

Regarding my report, may the Lord grant me grace to present the events as they occurred.

GENERAL REPORT

Thursday, May 17, 1951

On May, 17 1951, Brother Carlos Kozel—president of the General Conference of the Seventh Day Adventists, Reform Movement—gave opening to the conference at 9:00 A.M. as he opened with hymn number 1, followed by a short meditation from the Word of God and the welcoming of the delegates from the different Unions.

The following delegates were present:

German Union:

Br. Hartmann, Br. Fronz, Br. Luft, Br. Kissener and Br. S. Gutknecht (on May 7, Br. S. Gutknecht was not yet present).

Western European Union:

Br. A Ringelberg and Br. Mandemaker.

Southern European Union:

Br. A. Mueller and Sr. Luscher.

Scandinavian Union:

Br. E. Stara and Br. Helgerud.

Spanish Missionary Field:

Br. J. Escusa.

African Union:

Br. T. Buijs and Br. Tsotetsi.

North American Union:

Hno. D. Nicolici.

South American Union – Northern Division:

Br. Laicowski, Br. A. Craviotto and Br. C. Kozel.

South American Union – Southern Division:

Br. Cimera and Sr. R. Kozel.

Brazilian Union:

Br. Braga, Br. Lavrik, Br. Devay and Br. A. Cacan.

Australian Union:

Br. Steward.

The following brethren were permitted to be present in the meetings as translators and representatives, although without the right to vote:

Br. Blasius, Sr. L. Fritsch (France), Br. Eggarter (Austria), Br. M.P. Ringelberg, Br. Haven, Br. Bakker (Holland), Sr. Ferrari (Italy) and Sr. Craviotto (Argentina).

When I arrived a day later to the conference grounds, Br. Fronz quickly approached (also a delegate of our union) to inform me that certain difficulties arose during the first day on account of Br. D. Nicolici. These difficulties that arose, were also the reason why the General Assembly was anticipated from 1952 to 1951.

Br. Fronz's welcoming message was to me onerous. I considered it a great privilege to be sent as a delegate of a union to the General Conference Assembly, the greatest authority in the organization of the work of God. For me it was clear that neither I nor any of the delegates had the right to represent personal interests, but instead seek out that which was best for God's work. For this reason Br. Fronz told me not to allow Br. D. Nicoloci to influence me: "I will ask the Lord to grant eye salve that I may see and distinguish between righteousness and unrighteousness, truth and error."

After the opening of the General Conference Assembly the President of the General Conference required his secretary to read the minutes of 1948, the first General Assembly after World War II and the ban of our denomination.

To the consternation of the president of the meeting and the delegates, the secretary refused to read the report. Under the perspective of rights, divine order, and organization, Br. D. Nicolici made a fundamental error, which disqualified him as secretary and caused him to lose his office.

"God is a God of order;" such is the declaration of Paul, and according to divine organization and standard protocol of the denomination, a secretary is morally and juridically obliged to read the report, irrelevant to whether it pertains to the church, union, or conference. It was to be expected that a secretary of the General Conference would be a model of virtue, and with all manner of humility proceed in the reading of the report as to the request of the president, for only then could a good example be portrayed for the delegates that represented the entirety of the Reform work in the General Conference; naturally the aforementioned secretary had to have reasons for denying the reading of the report.

Although he was relatively young, and although this was his first time at the General Conference Assembly, it was incomprehensible for me to see how well he knew protocol and order, as much in the world as in the army and God's people; allowing a fundamental error to occur of such grave connotations regarding organization and order of the Lord and highest authority of administration in God's work.

The Sacred Scriptures offer us much evidence that reveal how much understanding our merciful God and Father has before our human weaknesses and imperfections, but if we portray an arrogant, proud, and insolent demeanor against God and His elected servants, then—as history has taught us—the subsequent consequences have been terrible. For reference I adjoin the following verses: Num. 16:1-5, 19-35; Deut. 17:12, 13; 1 Sam. 15:10-22.

"Now Korah, the son of Izhar, the son of Kohath, the son of Levi, and Dathan and Abiram, the sons of Eliab, and On, the son of Peleth, sons of Reuben, took men: And they rose up before Moses, with certain of the children of Israel, two hundred and fifty princes of the assembly, famous in the congregation, men of renown: And they gathered themselves together against Moses and against Aaron, and said unto them, Ye take too much upon you, seeing all the congregation are holy, every one of them, and the Lord is among them: wherefore then lift ye up yourselves above the congregation of the Lord? And when Moses heard it, he fell upon his face: And he spake unto

Korah and unto all his company, saying, Even to morrow the Lord will shew who are his, and who is holy; and will cause him to come near unto him: even him whom he hath chosen will he cause to come near unto him… And Korah gathered all the congregation against them unto the door of the tabernacle of the congregation: and the glory of the Lord appeared unto all the congregation. And the Lord spake unto Moses and unto Aaron, saying, separate yourselves from among this congregation, that I may consume them in a moment. And they fell upon their faces, and said, O God, the God of the spirits of all flesh, shall one man sin, and wilt thou be wroth with all the congregation? And the Lord spake unto Moses, saying, Speak unto the congregation, saying, Get you up from about the tabernacle of Korah, Dathan, and Abiram. And Moses rose up and went unto Dathan and Abiram; and the elders of Israel followed him. And he spake unto the congregation, saying, Depart, I pray you, from the tents of these wicked men, and touch nothing of their's, lest ye be consumed in all their sins. So they gat up from the tabernacle of Korah, Dathan, and Abiram, on every side: and Dathan and Abiram came out, and stood in the door of their tents, and their wives, and their sons, and their little children. And Moses said, Hereby ye shall know that the Lord hath sent me to do all these works; for I have not done them of mine own mind. If these men die the common death of all men, or if they be visited after the visitation of all men; then the Lord hath not sent me. But if the Lord make a new thing, and the earth open her mouth, and swallow them up, with all that appertain unto them, and they go down quick into the pit; then ye shall understand that these men have provoked the Lord. And it came to pass, as he had made an end of speaking all these words, that the ground clave asunder that was under them: And the earth opened her mouth, and swallowed them up, and their houses, and all the men that appertained unto Korah, and all their goods. They, and all that appertained to them, went down alive into the pit, and the earth closed upon them: and they perished from among the congregation. And all Israel that were round about them fled at the cry of them: for they said, Lest the earth swallow us up also. And there came out a fire from the Lord, and consumed the two hundred and fifty men that offered incense." Numbers. 16:1-5, 19-35.

"Wherefore it shall come to pass, if ye hearken to these judgments, and keep, and do them, that the Lord thy God shall keep unto thee the covenant and the mercy which he sware unto thy fathers: And he will love thee, and bless thee, and multiply thee: he will also bless the fruit of thy womb, and the fruit of thy land, thy corn, and thy wine, and thine oil, the increase of thy kine, and the flocks of thy sheep, in the land which he sware unto thy fathers to give thee." Deuteronomy 7:12, 13.

"Then came the word of the Lord unto Samuel, saying, it repenteth me that I have set up Saul to be king: for he is turned back from following me, and hath not performed my command-ments. And it grieved Samuel; and he cried unto the Lord all night. And when Samuel rose early to meet Saul in the morning, it was told Samuel, saying, Saul came to Carmel, and, behold, he set him up a place, and is gone about, and passed on, and gone down to Gilgal. And Samuel came to Saul: and Saul said unto him, Blessed be thou of the Lord: I have performed the commandment of the Lord. And Samuel said, What meaneth then this bleating of the sheep in mine ears, and the lowing of the oxen which I hear? And Saul said, They have brought them from the Amalekites: for the people spared the best of the sheep and of the oxen, to sacrifice unto the Lord thy God; and the rest we have utterly destroyed. Then Samuel said unto Saul, Stay, and I will tell thee what the Lord hath said to me this night. And he said unto him, say on. And Samuel said, When thou wast little in thine own sight, wast thou not made the head of the tribes of Israel, and the Lord anointed thee king over Israel? And the Lord sent thee on a journey, and said, Go and utterly destroy the sinners the Amalekites, and fight against them until they be consumed.19 Wherefore then didst thou not obey the voice of the Lord, but didst fly upon the spoil, and didst evil in the sight of the Lord? And Saul said unto Samuel, Yea, I have obeyed the voice of the Lord, and have gone the way which the Lord sent me, and have brought Agag the king of Amalek, and have utterly destroyed the Amalekites. But the people took of the spoil, sheep and oxen, the chief of the things which should have been utterly destroyed, to sacrifice unto the Lord thy God in Gilgal. And Samuel said, Hath the Lord as great delight in burnt offerings and sacrifices, as in obeying the voice of the Lord? Behold, to obey is better than sacrifice, and to hearken than the fat of rams." 1 Samuel 15:10-22.

Although I could not properly grasp the reason of such behavior, nevertheless it was evident that the man—who was the Secretary of the General Conference—had lost his office. When such a demonstration is made in audience of the representatives of the denomination the guilty party must be suspended of his appointment to reestablish order and respect before divine authority. Deuteronomy 17:12, 13.

I would ask myself what reasons he had, but it was later that I found that this man—during the terrible years of war, in which God's people had to suffer appallingly for the faith, being put into prisons and concentration camps, and many even gave their lives for the truth—was found in Australia, far from the cannonade and bombs.

The people of the Reform signed their faith and conviction of faithfulness to the Commandments of God with their blood. The ministers and the people, especially the youth, that were convinced of the message and wanted to remain faithful to their Lord had to follow their Savior to the valley of death. Several years after the war, while humanity still grieved the millions of injuries, the church scattered and persecuted experienced its resurrection, yet a new attack on this church so despised by the opposition was being formulated.

I was told that the previous secretary, Br. Rieck—who endured safely in Portugal during the war—and Br. Nicolici, in 1948, just three years after the world was ablaze, aspired to the highest office and wanted to instigate a rebellion. As they did not find supporters, Br. Reick remained in his obstinacy and separated from the denomination, while Br. Nicolici, on the contrary, tearfully showed "apparent" and sincere repentance, for which he was forgiven. As a testament of forgiveness he was elected as the secretary of the General Conference. This process with all of its affairs was written on the minutes, and as he was now secretary of the General Conference, he refused to read them, instead of being humble and sincere, therefore learning from this terrible experience and leaving for others a good example of humility.

Since in 1951 I experienced everything firsthand, with the help of God I wish to communicate everything as it truly happened in order to help the sincere souls of the Reform, that they may not be victims of the deceit by sweet words and false pretensions.

In the epistles of the apostle Paul and Peter we find words of warning: "But there were false prophets also among the people, even as there shall be false teachers among you, who privily shall bring in damnable heresies, even denying the Lord that bought them, and bring upon themselves swift destruction. And many shall follow their pernicious ways; by reason of whom the way of truth shall be evil spoken of. And through covetousness shall they with feigned words make merchandise of you: whose judgment now of a long time lingereth not, and their damnation slumbereth not." 2 Peter 2:1-3.

"For such are false apostles, deceitful workers, transforming themselves into the apostles of Christ. And no marvel; for Satan himself is transformed into an angel of light. Therefore it is no great thing if his ministers also be transformed as the ministers of righteousness; whose end shall be according to their works." 2 Corinthians 11:13-15.

During my first day I had to listen to the secretary and his constituents tell me that the head was sick (such were their thoughts towards the President of the General Conference, Br. C. Kozel). Br. Kissener was also strongly victimized, who was a delegate from the German Union and also had been a member of the committee during the last three years.

It was understandable at the time that everyone of us as delegates wanted first to listen to the reports of the different unions and mission fields, since we were interested in knowing how the work of God had spread throughout the world and which problems it was yet to face, hence we proceeded with organizational duties and future planning. Moreover, the precious time had to be used to establish good plans to push forward with greater success the work of God in the world. But in place of this the president was accused by his secretary. Br. Kissner and other brethren were also placed in the line of fire. This made it significantly clear that the behavior of this man in such an elevated office was irrevocable. This should have genuinely opened the eyes of anyone, if these representatives of the work of Christ would have allowed themselves to be guided by His Spirit and would have respected the established order.

The statements and accusations of the secretary against his president, Br. Korpmann—who from 1925 belonged to the Committee of the General Conference—and Br. Kissener were particularly poignant for me. I never expected nor would I have believed that something akin to this would be possible, since we do not meet to accuse each other; this broke from the schema that men and women of experience, sanctified by the Gospel of the cross, should learn humility from the Savior of the world, taking to heart the counsel of the apostle Paul: "but in lowliness of mind let each esteem other better than themselves." and "Bear ye one another's burdens, and so fulfil the law of Christ." Philippians 2:3, Galatians 6:2.

Regrettably, I could not confirm anything of this sort in that person or his constituents; this was naturally a strong deception for me as a young collaborator.

When the accusations continued the president of the General Conference—Br. C Kozel—requested to be allowed to resign from his office, which was approved by the majority of delegates in order to preserve the peace.

Although for me this step was incomprehensible according

to the organizational protocol (given that the president himself as well as his officials have to carry out their respective offices until these are laid down and through election the new administration is established in their stead), yet given the situation it can be understood.

Br. A. Ringelberg was elected as provisional president of the meetings. As delegates we believed that peace would return and the existing problems could be dealt with and regulated. We were wrong!

The next onslaught was directed at Br. Kissener. Although the case of brother Br. Kissener had already been dealt with in the Democratic Republic of Germany; the entire conference forgave him and in 1948 he was even elected as a member of the General Conference Committee. Now Br. D. Nicolici set all of his efforts to eliminate this brother also. It is of importance to note that Br. Nicolici wrote a letter to Br. Kissener before the General Assembly, encouraging him to remain in the committee because God had forgiven him his sin. Yet now, in the presence of all the brethren, his vitriol was aimed at Br. Kissener.

Br. Kissener did not wish that the Lord's work suffer, and for this reason he publicly declared that he would step down from his post as a delegate in order to protect the Lord's work for which he had suffered much. When it was made evident that the oral declaration was not enough for Br. D. Nicolici, Br. Kissener presented a written resignation letter in which stepped down as delegate of the German Union. Therefore the German Union counted on one less delegate, but this was also accepted to keep the piece.

In the meantime the unions presented some reports. The last

person to present the report was Br. D. Nicolici, on behalf of the American Union.

Some days before, Br. D. Nicolici had been attacking Br. Korpmann unceasingly. To all those who held responsibilities in the work of the Reform, as well as the brethren that had been under the leadership of Br. Korpmann in Estonia, Finland, and other Scandinavian countries, it was known that Br. Korpmann was a faithful and responsible brother. After the invasion of the Russians in Estonia Br. Korpmann had to flee and lost his wife in the process. After the war he tried to immigrate to Canada, which he was able to do. Although Br. Korpmann had been a member of the General Conference Committee since 1925, as was already stated, Br. D. Nicolici did not wish to even accept Br. Korpmann as a minister in the North American Union. Br. D. Nicolici accused Br. Korpmann to having a relationship with a sister from the "Big Church," this woman being divorced, but a letter arrived to the general conference session from the Canadian brethren, in which was stated that these accusations were false. It would have pleased Br. D. Nicolici that Br. Korpmann would have married this lady because she was rich; he wanted her money for the printing press he wanted to buy and establish in the U.S.A.

Friday May 18, 1951

On May 18, 1951, Nicolici spoke for three hours regarding the matter of Br. Korpmann and presented many accusations against him without being able to produce any proof of his accusations. Here I remember the testimony of the Spirit

EYEWITNESS

of Prophesy that I already cited in the beginning; accusations are worthless without proof. We had the impression that Br. D. Nicolici wanted to dispose of Br. Korpmann as a minister and member of the Committee of the General Conference, the reason being that he was too independent and was not in agreement with the leadership of the community. After three hours of accusations—which we had to endure patiently—Br. Korpmann stood, relaxed and peaceably, and said: "I have never seen such a liar," and sat back down.

Br. D. Nicolici used the morning hours with full knowledge, as to prevent Br. Korpmann from presenting the correct perspective of the matter; every judgment offers the accused the opportunity to defend himself, and when in worldly courts it is done so, how much more should this right be offered to a brother who proved his worth throughout many years of service for the Lord, undergoing tribulation and persecution. It was decided that Br. Korpmann would have such an opportunity on May 20, 1951 and in so doing respond to the accusations levied upon him and set the story straight. In Proverbs 10:17-19 an important warning is given for every child of God: "He is in the way of life that keepeth instruction: but he that refuseth reproof erreth. He that hideth hatred with lying lips, and he that uttereth a slander, is a fool. In the multitude of words there wanteth not sin: but he that refraineth his lips is wise."

No meetings took place on Friday evening, for these hours were set apart for preparation for the Sabbath. Br. D. Nicolici, but especially Br. Lavrik and other delegates of his union, were found in a very intense enterprise, revealing to other delegates their ideas and plans which they had set out to do. In so doing they sought to impair the trust held towards God's responsibility bearers.

Hitler outlawed the Reform in Germany and the properties confiscated. The brethren had to undergo ten years of bitter persecution, notwithstanding the remnant gathered once more at the end of the war, and with great joy the few workers together with the brethren began to work for the saving of souls. In a few years the work extended to more than a thousand members. As a result of the *Wirtschaftswunder*—the German economic miracle that took place after WWII—our organization held a healthy financial status. It was for this hidden agenda that Br. D. Nicolici, Br. Lavrik and others set their sights on the German Union and on convincing Br. Hartmann, Br. Fronz, Br. Eggarter, and myself. Rather than giving due diligence to preparation for the holy Sabbath, we were overwhelmed with propagandist material, not privy to the machinations of the givers.

Sabbath May 19, 1951

Sabbath arrived, May 19, 1951; it was received in customary fashion. The following morning we attended the Sabbath School and sermon, but in the afternoon we were once again lobbied with such an intensity that the Sabbath became no longer a day of joy and of exchange of ideas, but a very heavy psychological burden as a result of the current unrest.

As the Sabbath concluded Br. D. Nicolici initiated a dissertation in which he spent much time promoting his book on Revelation. Regarding this he presented the theory that we are the church of Philadelphia; this was something completely new for me, given that I had been taught by the Adventist Church that since the year 1844 we live in the period of Laodicea, in other words the seventh church. But Br. D. Nicolici had the unmitigated gall to declare and affirm in 1951 that we are the church of Philadelphia. Moreover, I was told that Sr. Nicolici had been revealed that Br. C. Kozel carried a dirty robe. These things opened my eyes and prompted me to keep a keen eye on the matter.

The Sabbath came to an end, we wished each other a blessed workweek, and I made my way to my quarters. We wished to have no contact with those—who with sweet words and pleasant promises—increasingly attempted to attract us to themselves.

Not much time passed before Br. Hartman—the representative of the president of the German Union—arrived heavily agitated and asked me to go with him to a very important meeting.

I was not expecting anything good to come from the events of Friday and Sabbath afternoon. I asked Br. Hartmann to leave me be, for I wanted to spend the hours alone with God in peace instead of conspiring in a nefarious plot; I simply refused to participate in a secret meeting. Hartmann urged me to go with him immediately a second time to this very important meeting. Even though Br. Hartmann was my superior, I once again refused to go because I saw in this the steps towards anarchy, but on account of his perseverance and the words of Br. Blasius (who slept in the same room): "Br. Hartmann is a brother of the Union, and for this reason I would go to listen as to the cause of such deliberation."

I let myself be persuaded and so I left, but when I noticed

that our path was found amidst the trees of the forest and it being a dark night, I was suddenly overcome my a thought and the Word of God in John 13:30: "He then having received the sop went immediately out: and it was night."

The thought of being a traitor was appalling; the psychological conflict that was ablaze in me was worse than advancing to my first Russian battlefront.

With each step we found ourselves deeper in the forest. It being a dark night, it was only at the last moment in which I saw a group of men gathered, as if awaiting someone or something. Br. Hartmann and I joined this group of Spanish and Portuguese speakers. At first I was intrigued and wished to know the purpose of our meeting in the darkness of the night, under the protection of the forest.

Thoughts raced through my mind and with each passing moment it was clearer to me that I had not lost anything for which I should be searching, and the Union had not granted me freedom to attend secret meetings nor to join in a conspiracy. I was hard pressed by the thought that in the political world such an action could be construed as a coup on the established order. One cannot dispense kisses and simultaneously drive the dagger into the back, nor can one speak of peace while surreptitiously preparing for war. This is deceit and hypocrisy.

I was finally informed that the purpose of the meeting was to sign a declaration, which was still being prepared by Br. D. Nicolici and Br. Steward of Australia. This was to be signed in this forest meeting under the cover of night. The troublemaker needed signatures; he needed to know how many of the delegates were willing on his side through the good and the bad.

EYEWITNESS

This news moved me much more. While this information was being revealed to me three men drew near. When the men beside me saw them they tried to flee—thinking that the leadership of the General Conference had sent people to investigate what was taking place in the forest—but it was not so. Three Brazilians were making their way to the meeting in order to wait and sign the aforementioned declaration together.

When I realized all this and came to know the impetus of the meeting, I took the word and said: "My brethren, we have been sent by the Union to deliberate the internal affairs of the General Conference. In accordance with democratic law we are free to express our opinion in the meetings as we seek the well being of the work. Through the reading of reports and the laying down of positions is found in the hands of the delegates to nominate someone who emanates trust for a position, yet everything is to be done with order, following due process, where the delegations are organized. Gathering signatures in a secret manner while tarnishing the conscience of the delegates is not divine, but satanic. The Lord God grants man the ability to choose freely. God does not force anyone into discipleship; the Lord does not seek to subdue, but attracts us with the cords of His everlasting love. As representatives of the people we must learn this lesson, and not only learn them but practice them here."

It was 11:00 P.M. and the declaration that was being drafted by Br. D. Nicolici and Br. Steward was not yet ready to be signed. I told the brethren there gathered that I would not nor could I ever do something thus. "I have not come to the church of God to embrace a rebellion, but I want to follow in the footsteps of the lamb and preach the good news." After my diatribe regarding my refusal to collaborate, the brethren reflected respectively. Since it was already deep into the night, I declared: "I'm going to my quarters"; two brethren followed me, but the rest, nevertheless, remained. Maybe they had already given their word and were waiting to sign the declaration.

I came to know the following morning that the declaration was not finished during the aforementioned night, but was instead signed at dawn by eleven delegates.

I left my room very early in the morning, sought out a tranquil scene, and with tears cried to God that he keep me from being snarled in any erroneous matter.

Sunday May 20, 1951

May 20, 1951 – 9:00 A.M.

Despite the surmounting tension present at the meeting, an undeniable peace seemed to be present when the board president gave opening to the day's session. It is noteworthy to point out that Br. D. Nicolici—who always carried the testimonies and the minutes of 1948—had no such articles with him on this morning, for he only carried a Bible.

As customary opening practice, the acting president called for the reading of Friday's minutes. There was an additional report in relation to the debate with the brethren from the United States, and finally Br. Steward, as temporary secretary, sandwiched the declaration and began to read. Since this was unknown to the president, being that he discovered certain signatures below, he interrupted the reading of the minutes and asked for clarification. He was told that it was a declaration.

A president that is loyal to order has to bind himself strictly to the program; for this reason the question was extended to the delegates whether they wanted to listen to a declaration. The voting resulted in the majority desiring for the reading of the document. A second question was extended to the delegates by the president, whether the reading should be carried out presently or after Br. Korpmann's defense, for this was the first matter on the agenda as decided on Friday. The delegates were not willing to set order aside, and the majority—except for those that had signed the declaration—voted in favor of Br. Korpmann stating his defense first and then reading the declaration. The voting was 13 in favor and 11 against.

Consequently, I did not vote, having already made an experience in the forest from Saturday night to early Sunday. Between the voting I desired to take the floor to clarify regarding the declaration, but unfortunately between the excitement of the delegates I was not given the opportunity to speak and for this reason I did not vote.

The "Goodbye"

But when the majority, nevertheless, voted in favor of Br. Korpmann presenting his defense and for the reading of the declaration to follow, Br. D. Nicolici arose from his seat, rose his hand as in greeting, uttered the words: "Goodbye" and left the hall; he was followed by eleven delegates and a translator, Br. Eggarter from Austria.

The two German delegates, Br. Hartmann (to my left) and Br.

Fronz (to my right) were seated next to me. When Br. D. Nicolici abandoned the hall and the others followed I asked Br. Hartmann and Br. Fronz to remain in the hall, for this was against divine order and the church. I continued by saying that the Union had trusted them and for this reason we should remain until the closure of the delegates meetings and election of officials.

Br. Hartmann turned and placed his hands on his head with awful excitement. Br. Fronz was more composed, but Br. Hartmann followed Br. D. Nicolici and abandoned the hall. Br. Fronz remained with me. We went to the restroom and conversed on why it was not acceptable to leave, for which reason Br. Fronz promised me that he would go in search of Br. Hartmann. I supported this plan and asked him to follow through, because we must all remain until the conclusion of the meetings.

Br. Fronz left and never returned; the separation was final. Initially a man sought to impair the trust through criticism and accusations, then he lured them with a promise to unite the hearts. In Proverbs 18:1 we read: "Through desire a man, having separated himself, seeketh and intermeddleth with all wisdom."

For the young generation I would like to point out that Br. Hartmann, after 16 years of strife against the church of God, returned with tears and spent the last years of his life within the flock of the Lord for whom he had previously worked and suffered. Br. Fronz, after a certain period of time, also abandoned the *Nicolici Group* and went to the Adventist Church. The same occurred with Br. Eggarter from Austria and his fellow countryman Br. Hohenrainer, who with soothsaying was swept into the same path and later also went to the Adventist Church. Br. Hohenrainer suffered a tragic death in an automobile accident, in which he fell into the river Drau; he tried to break the window with all his might before the car sank, but unfortunately was not able, so his life ended in that river. Br. Lavrik, who did the most service to Br. D. Nicolici in 1951, would go on to brand the president of his movement, Br. D. Nicolici, as a rebel and declared: "If Br. Nicolici is not a rebel then there is no rebellion." Nevertheless, he remained in the group and died in the movement.

After the Split

After the split, Br. Korpmann was given the opportunity to reply to the accusations of Br. D. Nicolici and to factually prove that the accusations spewed against him were false. As a result of this we were enlightened as to why Br. D. Nicolici wanted to avoid at all cost that Br. Korpmann have the opportunity to prove that those accusations were utter concoctions.

The fourteen remaining delegates were moved and wished that under no circumstances there might arise a split within the heart of the reform. A document was drafted and a delegate was sent to petition the brethren that had left to return; with the promise that the declaration would be read. Unfortunately, these attempts received with definite refusal. Another attempt was made, but it was also in vain; the answer was: "We shall not return."

These eleven delegates found a place, in the vicinity of the hotel where we were staying, where they conducted their meetings. When they reacted adversely to our invitations I went to their place of meeting and told those found present: "Brethren, the remaining delegates have emphasized on several occasions there desire to hear the declaration, and are striving to do anything to avoid any separation among God's people that will once again have to bear psychological suffering. The people of the Reform suffered enough in the previous war. As brethren and leaders we must do for Jesus all that is possible, having in mind John 17 to protect the people from these difficulties and problems of the soul." They also rejected me with a smile and clearly reiterated "NO" at the invitation to return.

Regrettably, I did not know that this small group had already—on Sunday May 20, 1951—organized and sent a telegraph to the treasurer and secretary of the German Union; Br. W. Egerter assured them everything: money, property, and literature.

But Br. W. Egerter, a faithful administrator of God's assets, did not allow himself to be confounded by false propaganda, but in turn closed all bank accounts, locked everything under lock and key, and came to Holland to establish for himself what had really happened. When we ascertained everything from Br. W. Egerter we were afraid and were then able to conclude that this scourge to the work of God was being prepared for a long time, but was just being executed. When Br. Egerter arrived in Holland and realized all that had happened, we decided to go together to that severed group and speak with Brs. Fronz and Hohenrainer, as well as the other brethren from the German union. Br. Hartmann, unfortunately, was no longer found in Holland, but was sent to drag down the German Union with him. We were able to speak with Br. Fronz and Br. Hohenrainer, to which we were informed that the elections had already occurred.

It was interesting to hear that the election of the president was carried out through the casting of lots, but when the lot fell on Br. Lavrik, it was cast again until Br. D. Nicolici, the orchestrator of the split, was elected president.

Naturally, this was a great disappointment for the two brethren, and during our conversation they were able to see that this could not be of God, but a doing entirely of men. We knelt, prayed, and all cried bitterly. These two brethren realized that this separation, the election process, the swift organization, and the attacks could never come from God; they promised to return the following day. The next day we waited for the return of the two brethren, but the wait was in vain. We tried to speak with them through the phone, but this too was hampered.

GENERAL QUESTIONS
Four Points to Consider

1. I have been and continue to be asked the question: "Who abandoned the place?" Once more I'd like to emphasize with clarity that eleven delegates and the translator abandoned the meeting hall and building in which we had the delegation meetings, and conducted their own organization meetings in an old and empty building nearby, yet they would return to the hotel for meals and to sleep; taking advantage of the hospitality of the Dutch. Holland was the hosting country and had committed to covering all expenses of this conference. Br. A. Ringelberg—president of the Dutch Field as well as the President of the General Conference—nor his committee could understand why they had to provide for these lodging and food, when these were had gone to other fields to steal away soles from the denomination.

I would like to place emphasis on this specific point that the delegates of the General Conference did everything possible to appeal to those that had left to return, as I have already explained. The Dutch Field, although they had already left, paid for their lodging and sustenance during the successive days.

But when through Br. W. Egerter we learned by writing that they wanted to take possessions through force and lobbied the brethren with false rumors and lies that they may be swayed in their favor, we left the locale and continued the meetings in the house of Br. A. Ringelberg.

The assertion that we left the place of meeting is not only a distortion of facts, but a conscious lie. I wish to reiterate again that Br. D. Nicolici and the ten abandoned the Conference on May 20 1951, and in spite of invitations and petitions to return, utterly refused, organized, and initiated a worldwide division. As all of the efforts, all of the petitions to return and collaborations were rejected, it is understandable that the hosts not want to financially support any further those that instigated the divide.

2. Another declaration through which believing souls have been deceived is that we excluded them. This accusation also fails to be true. As far as I can remember, the leaders: Br. D. Nicolici, Br. Lavrik, and Br. Laicowski were relieved of their posts only after their reiterated refusal upon the petition to return and after the organization of their group which cemented the irrevocable separation.

I think that every logical, responsible, and conscientious leader should have deposed his office when at the beginning Br. D. Nicolici refused to read the previous day's minutes. When the work of destruction was developing in plain sight, it was irresponsible to see everything and not act, but lament helplessly. Surely David wouldn't have done that; he protected his flock at the risk of his life, facing lions and bears. Even after he was anointed king, while still tending to the flock of his father, he came to know of the great danger that menaced the people of Israel by the hand of Goliath and the Philistines, when King

34

Saul had not the courage to face the blasphemer of the name of God, David rose in faith and trust and God conceded him a marvelous victory.

In the *Acts of the Apostles* we are informed that already in the first century A.D. cruel wolves would appear, who would only seek to destroy the flock of Jesus Christ. The Apostle Paul, full of the Holy Spirit, warned the leaders and the people with the following words: "For I have not shunned to declare unto you all the counsel of God. Take heed therefore unto yourselves, and to all the flock, over the which the Holy Ghost hath made you overseers, to feed the church of God, which he hath purchased with his own blood. For I know this, that after my departing shall grievous wolves enter in among you, not sparing the flock. Also of your own selves shall men arise, speaking perverse things, to draw away disciples after them." Acts. 20:27-30.

The disciple closest to Jesus, John, also writes in his second epistle about the many seducers that have existed in this world and warned the church with the words: "Look to yourselves, that we lose not those things which we have wrought, but that we receive a full reward." In verses 10 and 11 he declares: "If there come any unto you, and bring not this doctrine, receive him not into your house, neither bid him God speed: For he that biddeth him God speed is partaker of his evil deeds." 2 John 8:10, 11.

Precisely in our time, when the testimonies speak of winds of doctrine, we need to be aware lest we become victims of the wiles of Satan. According to Revelation 12:17, Satan will direct his wrath precisely against those who constitute the reform the keeps the commandments of God and has the faith of Jesus Christ.

3.   The accusation that we have changed principles relating to the matter of matrimony is not justifiable, being that before the split no subject matter was discussed in relation to principle, for the delegates had only presented their reports.

When someone subscribing to an extreme point of view has the fear that someone amongst the delegates present the request that the innocent party can remarry, being that the Adventist pioneers held this view, basing their belief on two letters written by Sr. E.G. White, which offers the advice that the innocent party remains free to contract matrimony; one should wait for such a petition to be made and a decision taken.

When this thought was presented in 1956 it was rejected by the delegates, because we are not all-knowing and it is extremely difficult to determine which is the guilty party. Precisely because we know of the great need in this field and because the devil has succeeded in destroying the happy home—separating marriages, leaving children without parents and a home—we advice every young man and woman to meditate seriously first, calling unto God often regarding the partner with whom they are to unite for their entire life. One must first know if one is willing to live with the partner for such a time as death do ye part. Furthermore, it is very important to be willing to ask forgiveness and to forgive the faults of the spouse. It is only when the love of God joins two people, and not just the love *eros*, the physical impulse to contract marriage, that the conditions are met so that marriage and a family remain intact.

4.   It continues to be said that there is no desire for reconciliation from our behalf, but on the contrary, for this declaration is incorrect and secondly, confusing for the brethren that are not always in the task of examining the true matter. It is a fact that in Holland in 1951 we did everything at our disposal to avoid a separation and subsequently, when I was elected President of the General Conference, set the objective, with the grace of God and His help, to end this war between brethren and heal the bloody wound.

Since the fundamental question has yet to be addressed, the question always arises as to why a separation occurred and whether there were fundamental reasons or whether the separation was a result of self interests that led to a catastrophe which caused the faith of so many to crumble, marriages and families to breakup, the consequences being pain and tears. Thus the only way to follow the path of the prodigal son would be to say: "I will arise and go to my father..." Luke 15:18. This would be the right path and the correct behavior before God and the people.

The 1967 Unification Talks

When I was urgently asked in 1966 to take the responsibility of the work, after two days of reflection and serious prayers, I finally accepted, called to God, and prayed: "Lord if it is amongst Your plans that I take on the responsibility of the General Conference, then grant me your grace that this crack which has arisen amongst your people may be closed. I want to do everything in my power to work for this cause."

When it was known that I was elected president, brethren from the *Nicolici Movement*: Dr. Canyo from Yugoslavia, Br. Cidric of Australia, Br. Barath from Brasil, Br. B. Cholich from the United States, and Br. Nicolici contacted me to propose unity among God's people.

In 1967 the *Nicolici Movement* had its General Assembly in Brazil and a proportion of the delegates pressured to come into contact with us and formed a committee of peace to present to the union. When I was presented this request, I tried to discuss it with my advisors. Despite the bitter experiences we had made in the past, the brethren saw, nevertheless, the need to try everything to reach a unity.

I formed a delegation committee of three brethren: the secretary of the General Conference, Br. Ringelberg, the treasurer of the General Conference, Br. W. Egerter, and the president of the South American Division, Br. A. Craviotto to send them to Brazil to speak with the committee of peace to seek a path to unity. At first it seemed that the union was very close. On our side, we were not only willing to forgive and forget, but were even willing to preserve their Bible workers and all who held office in the *Nicolici Movement*, but they would have to recognize that the separation was not pleasing to God, nor was it just. Thus, joined together in the love of the Lord we would dedicate ourselves to our work, the evangelization of the world.

Unfortunately, after six weeks of hard work, several delegates informed us that behind closed doors the contrary was being decided, and that it was only orchestrated as a trap for us. To great disdain, it only cost us time and money without being able to reach any goal.

It is of importance to note that Br. D. Nicolici publically recognized his guilt, as well as Br. Laicowski and those that took part in the separation that took part in 1951; who wanted to finally free their conscience by declaring that it was wrong to separate without a reason. There were powers behind all of this that controlled the whole scene and prevented a union. I would later come to know that the greatest opponents of the union were Br. Volpp, Br. Balbacas, and Br. Sass. This is very sad, because if the union had occurred there would have been great joy in heaven and among the brethren, who nevertheless suffered much on the cause of the split.

A pioneer of the Reform Movement and experienced leader, and during that time a teacher at the missionary school, told us the students: "Rebellion is like a cadaverous venom, it's lethal."

I attempted another reconciliation in Yugoslavia when Br. Hartmann, after 16 years working against us, returned. Br. Hartmann, Br. Egerter, who served as a delegate in the 1967 peace, and myself traveled to Yugoslavia to extend the hand of reconciliation, but when we arrived and made our way to their headquarters in Moravska, Br. Volpp as well as Br. Bosanats appeared and prohibited Br. Hartmann from speaking. Br. Egerter was also unable to speak and only I was able to say a few words, to which I was responded with: "Well, if you want something make your way to our General Conference."

I could only ask God to forgive me, for in spite of my personal experiences in 1951, which caused time and money, I made another attempt. But I find comfort in the Lord, the Searcher of hearts, who knows the motives better than anyone.

For love and compassion towards the innocent souls that have fallen into this misery with the hope that there existed a possibility of reconciliation and union among the people who pretend to believe in God and in the truth, who also pretend to know the Bible and the testimonies; for this reason I have taken this to paper. Regrettably, I had to suffer a bitter disappointment and make the same experience that Moses and Aaron made with Korah. May God open the eyes of every sincere soul and lead them to the true flock of Jesus.

S. Gutknecht.

www.ingramcontent.com/pod-product-compliance
Lightning Source LLC
Chambersburg PA
CBHW070326160726
47999CB00003B/1178